RESTAURANT MANAGER'S
POCKET HANDBOOK

PURCHASING &
INVENTORY

25 KEYS TO

Profitable
Success

DAVID V. PAVESIC, F.M.P.

Copyright© 1999 by David V. Pavesic, Ph.D.
Lebhar-Friedman Books

Lebhar-Friedman Books is a company of Lebhar-Friedman Inc.

Printed in the United States of America

Library of Congress Cataloging-in-Publication Data

Pavesic, David V.
    Restaurant manager's pocket handbook : 25 keys to
profitable success. Purchasing & inventory / David V.
Pavesic.
        p.   cm.
    Includes index.
    ISBN 0-86730-756-0 (pbk.)
    1. Food service purchasing.   2. Food service--Inventory
control.   I. Title.
TX911.3.P8P38   1998
647.95'068'7--dc21   98-39302
                                                          CIP

PURCHASING & INVENTORY are central to the operations of any restaurant. An operator must know how much was purchased and on hand to be able to analyze the sale of menu items for theft, spoilage, and overportioning. The price and quality of products purchased will be reflected in the prices charged and profits earned. Keep in mind that price paid and quality are directly related.

The purveyor-operator relationship must be built upon mutual respect and understanding of each other's goals and objectives; one needs the other for survival. Both are businesses seeking to provide goods and services to their customers, and each struggles with the same problems and issues germane to the business world. But sometimes both parties lose sight of that fact and make life extremely difficult for each other. When they work together for their mutual benefit, though, the transacting of business proceeds smoothly and efficiently.

Inventory is not just a once-a-month exercise performed for accounting purposes. Inventory records are a critical element of any cost-control program. Inventory is too important to be reduced to mental records or hastily written notes on some yellow legal tablet. With the transient nature of the work force — and that includes management — a written inventory is absolutely necessary for the continuity of the purchasing process.

As foodservice professionals, we must demand a higher standard and accountability in purchasing and inventory activities. Because the inventory process is so critical, we must establish procedures that can be performed quickly and accurately. That calls for organization and systemization of the purchasing and inventory process.

Effective purchasing will result in the correct products being available when required, in the proper amounts, and at the best price relative to quality and service. The selection of purveyors is one that requires review of many more factors than just the price quoted.

PURCHASING & INVENTORY

Written inventory records are an essential element of your purchasing and inventory controls

YOUR PURCHASING STRATEGY is an integral component of the overall business plan because it directly impacts profit margins, cash management, asset turnover, and return on investment. Efficient purchasing permits costs to be lowered without a corresponding decrease in quality or portion sizes. Cost stability means menu prices remain stable and more competitive than those of operators who "ride the market" weekly.

Written records are critical if you want to have an effective food-cost control program. Written purchase and inventory records are just as important as the guest check. Written purchase and inventory records are just as important as your sales reports and guest checks. An operation that doesn't keep written inventory records because the owner or manager "keeps it all in his head" is like the chef who doesn't put recipes in writing. Those restaurant owners really don't know their "true" costs. And there's cause for concern when a manager or chef leaves the operation or even is out sick or goes on vacation. Without written records those left in charge will struggle to determine what, how much, and from whom to order.

The likelihood of a manager being transferred, fired, or quitting is highly probable, and the ordering function must proceed uninterrupted. There is no period of adjustment for purchasing when managers are transferred to a unit in another city or state. But if adequate written inventory records have been kept, the ordering function will remain a smooth and efficient process.

The information contained in the inventory records should include: the names of the primary and secondary suppliers; the product description or specifications; the unit of purchase and the price paid; and a record of the use levels between deliveries. If such detailed written records are kept, anyone who understands the system quickly can determine what needs to be purchased, from whom, how much to pay, and how much to order.

The use levels between deliveries are ascertained by noting the differences between successive amounts of stock on hand plus order quantities. For example, if there were three cases of tomato sauce (six No. 10 cans per case) on hand on Jan. 7 and five cases were ordered, a total of eight cases were available. If on Jan. 14, there were two cases on hand, the use level must have been six cases.

Take inventory often

HOW OFTEN should you take inventory? The answer depends on your purpose for taking inventory. Technically, you need to take inventory as frequently as you order. So if you order produce five times a week, you should inventory produce five times a week. When it comes to a fiscal inventory — that is, counting everything on hand and extending the value of the stock on hand — you should do that at least once a month for accounting purposes. Some operators take weekly inventory to keep on top of food and beverage costs, especially if they've been having a problem.

Some operators take inventory after each meal period to pinpoint product theft, but once a month is enough to calculate the cost of goods consumed for the income statement. When you take inventory before calling in an

> **"Few people are successful unless a lot of other people want them to be."**
>
> — Charles Brower

order to a supplier, you do it to determine the amount required. The amount you need to order depends on how much you have on hand and how much you will use between successive deliveries.

Still other operators take a fiscal inventory only once a year, which is all that is necessary for income tax purposes. But the operators who take a fiscal inventory only annually have no idea what their food cost is running the other 11 months of the year. That was the practice at a restaurant I worked for early in my management career. Although monthly income statements and balance sheets were prepared, food cost was based on inputting an average inventory figure. That practice, while quick and easy, offered no help in evaluating food cost and detecting waste and theft. Eventually, they changed that practice and instituted a monthly fiscal inventory.

I've learned over time that not taking a monthly fiscal inventory is fairly common among many independent operators. There's a fallacy in that logic, even if the operation generates the same amount of sales volume every month and the menu-sales mix remains the same — neither of which is a realistic expectation. Using an average inventory every month will over- or understate the value of the month-end inventory. The reason? While inventory is taken on the last day of the month, the day of the week on which the month ends will vary from one month to the next, and that will change the amount of inventory on hand.

Consider how much inventory can vary just by the day of the week. Your storeroom and walk-ins probably will be filled to capacity on Friday and Saturday, while Sunday and Monday will likely find their contents depleted. Remember: To calculate the cost of food consumed for the income statement, you must subtract your ending inventory from the total of your beginning inventory plus your purchases for the month. If you undervalue your ending inventory, it will increase the cost of food consumed, and you will run a higher food-cost percentage. If you overvalue your inventory, you will decrease the cost of food consumed and run a lower food-cost percentage. If you're paying corporate income taxes on a quarterly basis, you might be overstating your taxable income or underpaying what you owe.

Another practice operators use instead of taking a monthly fiscal inventory is to use total food purchased for the month as the cost of food consumed. That is equally ineffective in detecting theft and waste and doesn't provide management with accurate food-cost figures. Consider that food purchases are not an expense until they are consumed. The unused inventory is still a current asset on your balance sheet. A delivery received on the next-to or last day of the month probably won't be consumed before the end of the month and therefore isn't an expense in the accounting sense. If you use your food purchases for the month as the food-cost figure on your income statement, you will overstate your cost of food consumed. That will reduce your profit for the month and hide the true food-cost activity.

With a little organization of your inventory records and storage areas, the inventory process can be made an efficient and painless process. One should approach inventory taking with the same intensity and attention given to counting each day's sales receipts. The process of counting everything on hand should not take more than two hours, depending on the size of the restaurant. The extension of the value of inventory may take another two hours if extended manually or just seconds if extended with a computer. Just remember: There are no shortcuts for accuracy in inventory. You must count every item and extend its value.

Separate nonfood items when you are totaling inventory figures

IN ADDITION TO TAKING frequent inventories, the items you include in your total inventory can make a great deal of difference in your food costs at the end of the month. Consider all the nonfood items you keep on hand: cleaning supplies, dishwasher chemicals, and detergents; carryout boxes, bags, and containers; plastic wrap and aluminum foil; mop heads; paper napkins; replacement china, silver, and glassware; liquor, beer, and wine. If, by accident or design, such nonfood items are included in the total food inventory figures, the inventory will be overstated significantly and will lower the cost of food consumed. That will understate your food-cost percentage for the accounting period.

While most operators would not include liquor, beer, and wine in their food inventory,

"I find that the harder I work, the more luck I seem to have."

— THOMAS JEFFERSON

---

that is not always the case with nonfood supplies. Consider that you feasibly could have more than $1,000 in dishwasher chemicals if you received a delivery the last week of the month. If that was included in your food inventory, it would lower your cost of food consumed considerably. That is one of the first things I look for when reviewing month-end inventory figures. If nonfood items are included in the total, they must be deducted.

In fast-food operations where disposable containers and sandwich wrap are part of every hamburger or sandwich sold, paper supplies often are treated just like food cost. The counting of paper cups, Styrofoam sandwich clam shells, and french fry boxes are critical elements of sales-revenue control. While such items must be part of the monthly inventory records, separating them from food inventory is recommended. Counting nonfood inventory as food makes it more difficult to narrow down where your costs are out of line.

When I review financial statements and question the food-cost figures that are being reported, a glance at the balance sheet can shed light on the accuracy of the income statement numbers. Remember: Inventories of food, beverage, and supplies are assets in the accounting sense and should be shown in the current asset section of the balance sheet. If there is only one figure for inventory, it suggests that the food expense could be understated and the food inventory overstated. I expect to see separate inventory figures for food, beverages, and supplies. In fact, I recommend that even alcoholic beverage inventory values be separated for beer, wine, liquor, and even bottled waters. When no inventory is shown in the current assets, you should question the accuracy of the income statement's bottom line.

For cost-analysis purposes, it's always better to break down inventory — and costs — into separate categories rather than to group them together into one figure. You always can add up the separate totals if you want; however, when you have only one aggregate inventory figure to work with and require a detailed breakdown for each separate area, you must go back to the inventory records or individual ledger-account balances to obtain the figures. Instruct your accountant to assign each category a separate line-item identification.

(1) What is the minimum number of times inventory needs to be taken for accounting purposes?

  A. Once a week
  B. Once a month
  C. Once a year
  D. Once a day
  E. As often as you order

(2) How often should you take inventory for purposes of ordering from purveyors?

  A. Once a week
  B. Once a month
  C. Once a year
  D. Once a day
  E. As often as you order

(3) Which of the following is not part of your written inventory records?

  A. Primary and secondary purveyors
  B. Product specifications
  C. Standardized recipe
  D. Use levels between deliveries
  E. Unit of purchase

(4) Which of the following is the smaller amount in dollar value?

  A. Cost of food sold
  B. Cost of food consumed

(5) Substituting either your monthly food purchases or using an "average" monthly inventory as your cost of food consumed is a recommended practice in lieu of taking a fiscal inventory.

  A. True
  B. False

ANSWERS: 1: B, 2: E, 3: C 4: A, 5: B

Organize your records to expedite taking inventory and improve the accuracy of the analysis

ONCE YOU HAVE COMPILED a written inventory record, the way it is organized can improve your ability to ascertain quickly and accurately what and how much you must order. The inventory book should be set up by storage areas — dry storage, refrigerated storage, freezer storage, and so on. The order in which items are listed on the respective pages should correspond to the order in which they're placed on the shelves. Typically, similar items are stored near one another. For example, in my storeroom all tomato products — tomato sauce, crushed tomatoes, and tomato puree — were stored in sequence. Next to them were the canned vegetables, such as green beans, garbanzo beans, and kidney beans. A similar grouping was made for spices and herbs, condiments, and salad dressings.

That organization allowed items to be counted quickly and transferred to the inventory records without having to skip lines or move around the storeroom. It was especially appreciated when we were counting the items in the freezer during the cold winter months. By having the inventory records kept by product groups and storage areas, it made for easy analysis at the end of the month. We discovered that 60 percent of our food inventory value was kept in our walk-ins, not in dry storage. Our controls were increased in the those areas because that is where we had the most to lose.

We organized the storeroom so that everything was put in the same place every week. We placed signs on the shelves so that employees would know where an item was to be stored. That simple organization eliminated the problem of assuming an item was out of stock when in fact it had been stored in the wrong place. That system makes the regular weekly inventory process an efficient and easy task. The month-end fiscal inventory process can be expedited by having separate pages for prepared foods like cut steaks and cooked sauces. Remember: When taking a complete fiscal inventory, you must count all food items, including the condiments in the dining room and the herbs, opened spices, and other food supplies used in the kitchen.

Take inventory on the same day every week to determine your use levels between deliveries

ONE OF THE MOST IMPORTANT bits of information that you obtain from taking inventory regularly is your use levels of specific ingredients. That information is critically important in determining how much you must keep on hand to get from one delivery to the next. Each of your suppliers will have different order and delivery days, so you must organize your purchasing system to meet your schedule first and not be inconvenienced by suppliers' schedules. One solution is to take inventory on the same day(s) every week.

I used to take my weekly inventory every Sunday evening to make up my orders for the following week. Orders were given on Monday and Tuesday, with deliveries arriving on Tuesday and Wednesday for nonperishable items. Perishable items, such as seafood, meat, and poultry were ordered a minimum of twice a week, while items like produce and dairy products were delivered three to four times each week. The quantities ordered were based on the frequency of delivery, how much we had on hand, and how much we would use between deliveries.

Once you settle into a regular order-delivery schedule, you can organize your work days more efficiently. You're prepared for heavy delivery days and can schedule staff to help check deliveries and place items into storage. The same holds true for placing orders to your suppliers. Orders are called in or given to sales representatives at set times of the day, which allows management to move on to other matters requiring their attention.

Some operators use a par-stock level to determine how much to order and keep on hand. To determine a par stock, you estimate the use level of the busiest week of the year and then add a small safety factor. That becomes your par inventory.

In my restaurants in Florida, the winter tourist season was our busiest, and our inventory almost doubled over what we normally kept on hand during the rest of the year. If we based our inventory par stocks on how much we used during our peak months, we would have far too large an inventory, tie up our limited storage space, and increase our accounts payable. With inventory records that allowed us to determine the actual use levels between deliveries, we ordered only what we were likely to use between deliveries plus a small safety factor.

How should inventory be 'valued' at the end of the month?

I STATED PREVIOUSLY that you must take inventory at least once a month for accounting purposes. The counting and extending of the value of the food, supplies, and beverages on hand is referred to as a "fiscal" inventory. Fiscal denotes a budgetary, financial, or monetary exercise. The term "fiscal" often is expressed as "physical," which can mean material or tangible. Both imply counting and extending the value of inventory.

One of the most important aspects of arriving at a dollar value for the total ending inventory is assigning a cost to each of the items in stock. The price paid for many of the items is likely to have increased during the month. That is especially true for perishables like fresh produce, fresh meats, and seafood. The question then is, "Which of the purchase prices should

> **"Flaming enthusiasm, backed by horse sense and persistence, is the quality that most frequently makes for success."**

— DALE CARNEGIE

be used to value the unused inventory?" Your accountant will recommend several ways to value your inventory and the one he or she recommends will be determined by your particular tax bracket and the market dynamics affecting supply and price.

In a rising or inflationary economic climate, the first-in-first-out, or FIFO, method would increase the value of your ending inventory and lower your cost of food consumed and overall food-cost percentage. That would raise your gross profit and income-tax obligations. The opposite inventory-valuation method would be the last-in-first-out method, or LIFO. The last items purchased, usually at higher prices, are assumed to be the first sold. That leaves the lower-priced items purchased earlier in inventory. That is the recommended method when taxes or inflation rates are high, and one wants to minimize taxes payable. If prices for food and supplies are increasing, and you calculate the value of your ending inventory based on the earliest prices paid, you will reduce the total value of your ending inventory, increase your cost of food consumed and overall food-cost percentage, and reduce your profit and income taxes payable. By using LIFO, inflationary effects and phantom profits are reduced, and cash flow is improved.

Most operators don't give inventory valuation much thought and simply use the most recent price paid to value the inventory. No consideration is given to tax implications whatsoever. LIFO works to your benefit when you have had a good year. If you're having a bad year, LIFO will cause you to show a loss. LIFO is not recommended when you're submitting financial statements for a loan or when you're reporting to investors. The Internal Revenue rules and regulations do allow you to value inventory differently for balance-sheet purposes than for income-statement purposes. The way it is treated for income-statement purposes is to reduce the value of inventory to increase the cost of food sold, so there will be less taxable profit. On the other hand, if you wanted to emphasize the financial solvency of the operation to prospective investors, franchisees, or buyers, you would want to show a strong asset position. And if prices were rising, FIFO would be the better approach to inventory valuation.

Although food, beverages, and supplies are only assets as long as they're not used, the current asset position can be enhanced by valuing our inventory in such a way as to increase its value. Many lenders want to see a strong current ratio (current assets divided by current liabilities) and quick ratio (liquid current assets divided by current liabilities). Those ratios are used to assess the operation's ability to meet current obligations when they come due. Value your inventory the way that is financially sound for your operation.

Know the prerequisites and objectives of the purchasing function and the channels of distribution to the foodservice industry

THE FOOD MARKETING CHAIN begins with the agricultural producers. Only a small percentage of the total number of restaurant operators purchase directly from growers, farmers, and ranchers. The majority of the products purchased in commercial foodservice operations come from distributors who deal directly with processors, manufacturers, and fabricators. Those entities take the raw, unprocessed fruits, vegetables, meat, poultry, and seafood and process them into forms that the restaurateur utilizes. Fabricators take products from farmers and wash, trim, wrap, cook, can, freeze, or package fresh for use in commercial and institutional foodservice operations. However, they don't normally sell directly to the restaurant operator.

After processing has been completed, the products are handled by intermediaries in the distribution channel. Those are the purveyors, distributors, and suppliers that sell directly to the restaurant operations. Some are referred to as full-service wholesalers or total suppliers because they offer the convenience of one-stop shopping and sell everything from canned goods and fresh meats to china, glassware and cleaning supplies. But while those giants carry a broad line of items, they carry a limited number of grades, sizes, and brands.

Specialty suppliers are firms that don't carry a broad line of products but offer a great depth and variety of their specialty items. Examples are meat and seafood wholesalers. If you want to sell top-quality seafood, beef, pork, or lamb, for example, you will find what you need from the specialty supplier.

Working for the manufacturers, processors, fabricators, and wholesalers are brokers and manufacturer's representatives. The broker represents and promotes the products from one or more of the processors or manufacturers. They don't sell the product directly to the end user; instead, they support the sales representatives and wholesalers who do. The broker often calls on a restaurant operator and conducts product demonstrations or offers product samples. If the operator likes the products, the broker will refer him to the local wholesaler to obtain the product. Manufacturer's representatives differ from brokers in that they carry an inventory of products and deliver them to suppliers or end-users.

Quality and value recognition are prime requisites of good purchasing. You must be certain you have the best products and price for your specific needs. A buyer must know what constitutes quality and be able to recognize it if he or she is to make effective price comparisons when bids are obtained. Commercial food buying has two approaches: the requirements of the operation and the availability of products on the market. Certainly, there are times when you are happy to get any product, whatever the price or brand. The buyer might have to begin with the products that are obtainable in the market area, which could mean that menu adjustments must be made and preparation methods changed to fit product availability. In fact, products purchased are often a compromise between need and availability. But compromises can be reduced by knowing the availability of specific products in your market. With the great efficiencies in preservation and transportation, just about any product is obtainable in any part of the country at any time of the year.

The farther ahead you can forecast your order quantities, the better you can negotiate price with your suppliers. Depending too heavily on spot purchasing can be a big mistake. Spot buying is what most operators do when they call their seafood or meat suppliers and ask them to quote prices for the coming week.

If you can contract for future supply at a specified price, you can   protect yourself against sudden and unexpected product-cost increases. Typically, menu prices are not updated more than twice a year; therefore, they must account for the cost differentials that will occur from the normal supply-and-demand cycle throughout the year.

> **"Obstacles are those frightful things you see when you take your eyes off your goal."**
>
> — HENRY FORD

As a buyer, you should discuss the options your suppliers might offer that can reduce the risk of unexpected price fluctuations that occur when you spot purchase. Those options are cost-plus, contract prices, commissary system, and cooperative purchases.

With cost-plus the buyer negotiates to pay a specific markup over the supplier's cost — thus the name cost-plus buying. The benefit of cost-plus is that the prices paid are lower than the normal markup quoted on spot purchasing. That kind of buying can be negotiated by both independent and chain-restaurant accounts.

Corporate chains like Red Lobster were quick to realize the savings that could be obtained by eliminating the middleman in the flow of seafood from the docks to their restaurants. Red Lobster was one of the first companies to contract with commercial fishing fleets and establish its own source of supply, assuring a stability of delivery. As a result, the chain was able to pass on the savings to its customers in the form of lower prices.

Some small chains and groups of independent operators consolidate their purchasing by buying direct from processors and manufacturers. To do so effectively, they must purchase in quantity and then take delivery at one location and deliver to their own units. That is called a commissary system. But that method is limited in application to items shipped in bulk and already fully prepared and processed. If processing is required, the facility must comply with USDA standards, especially if product is shipped interstate. Additional savings are realized by eliminating the markup that would be attached to the product if supplied by a distributor. However, the markup includes delivery charges and warehousing expenses. Those expenses must be assumed by the company operating the commissary. Most chains have abandoned the warehousing of bulk items, as the cost savings often are negated by the costs of warehousing and delivery.

Still others seeking to reduce acquisition costs employ what is referred to as cooperative buying. That occurs when a group of independent operators or chain affiliates consolidate their purchasing and negotiate with suppliers for all members' business. Those purchasing groups give single-unit independents the same buying power of multiunit chains and help the small operators compete with the giants. Such groups have been successful in the institutional sector. But while the advantages of such an arrangement are evident, costs are involved. Someone must be entrusted with the responsibility of selecting suppliers, negotiating prices, and terms. Members also must concede that their choices of suppliers will be restricted for them to receive the cost savings.

The buying group concept has mixed success in the commercial foodservice industry. If such a group is to work, members must use the program. And it might be too much to ask independent operators and private, member-owned clubs to break from tradition — even when it is financially beneficial to do so. While the value of co-op purchasing is certainly valid and useful, the co-op must be more than self-sustaining.

What a buyer must know in order to make the right purchasing decisions

REMEMBER: Purchasing is an administrative function requiring both knowledge of the products and services and an understanding of the market dynamics that affect availability and price. It entails making decisions about specific brands, grades and types of products, and the purveyors who will supply them. The ordering function is simply determining the quantities. Ordering can be delegated, but not purchasing decisions. In multiunit chains the purchasing decisions are made at the corporate level. Usually a corporate-purchasing agent is responsible for securing contracts from suppliers at predetermined prices. Suppliers seeking your company's business will call upon corporate administrators, not unit managers.

In order to carry out the purchasing function and control costs, the operator must accurately forecast an operation's sales and menu-sales mix. Only then will he know what and how much the restaurant must have on hand. He also must establish and adhere to product specifications, enforce the use of standardized recipes to obtain standard yields, monitor portioning, and minimize waste. Once those elements are under control, the operator can purchase and prepare accurately in accordance with sales forecasts.

The person responsible for purchasing decisions should be able to judge if a distributor is quoting a fair price. Knowledge of market cycles and seasonal variations in quality and price of products purchased is important. A buyer must check the market regularly to learn of new product lines.

A buyer must understand how the prices paid at the primary markets will affect the prices charged by secondary and local sources. Subscribing to the various U.S. Department of Agriculture market reports can assist you in determining whether local distributors are quoting fair prices. The buyer cannot rely exclusively on supply and demand information received from sales reps. Understanding grading terminology, labeling terms, and standards used to judge quality also is a basic requirement.

Knowledge of the growing seasons and how to "read the market" for signs of supply, demand, and price fluctuations can be valuable also. The greater the probability of price and supply uncertainty, the greater the need to monitor the marketplace. A buyer's responsibilities go far beyond just getting the best price; standards of quality must be upheld as well.

Purchasing techniques improve your buying efficiency

9

A COMBINATION OF DIFFERENT methods of purchasing typically are utilized by buyers in commercial foodservice operations. The methods are sometimes classified as being either formal or informal. When contact between the buyer and seller is made over the phone or face-to-face, it is referred to as open or informal buying. Terms and negotiations are expressed orally.

Formal buying, on the other hand, employs written specifications and agreed-upon terms are put in writing. Formal buying is the norm for chain operations for which cost and quality control are critical to product standards. However, independent operators also can enter into formal buying agreements with suppliers.

Two examples of informal buying methods are open-market or market-quotation buying.

Those methods are practiced weekly by operators who call around on Monday morning to get the current prices. Sales representatives call upon each of their accounts to quote prices and take orders. This method assumes that the supplier who quotes the lowest price will get the order.

Chain operations that require large quantities of product realize that open-market purchasing isn't really cost effective. Consequently, large quantity users contract in "futures" for such items as ground beef and french fries. That involves a contractual agreement on both the price to be paid and the quantity to be supplied. The order must be "locked up" so that the operator is assured he will have sufficient product at an acceptable price. That method stabilizes costs and allows an operator to maintain menu prices over longer periods of time.

The objective in a formal purchasing agreement is to take the guesswork out of the ordering process. Once product specifications have been agreed upon, the only thing the buyer must do is arrange for those products to be delivered in the quantities ordered. That relieves the unit managers of time-consuming telephone calls and allows them to spend more time on important operational issues.

Consolidate your buying power

10

IF YOU OPERATE THREE OR MORE units, you can consolidate your buying power by negotiating for all of your units through your main office rather than having each unit manager make individual purchasing decisions. Designate one person to negotiate prices, delivery, and payment terms on all products and services. Doing so requires that you establish standard purchase specifications for all of your units. You gain cost and quality consistency when you consolidate your purchasing power.

As the general manager of a five-unit family restaurant chain in Kansas City, Mo., I learned early that unit managers and purveyor sales representatives were not evenly matched. Each unit general manager typically would call around to get prices and purchase from the supplier with the lowest price. But several prob-

"Opportunities multiply as they are seized."

— Sun Tzu

---

lems were revealed when all units submitted a fiscal inventory. Not only did we discover that different brands and grades of products were being used, but also prices paid varied and purveyors charged different prices for the same items.

Needless to say, that infuriated several of the managers. "Why shouldn't we all pay the same low price?" they demanded. My reply was that we should and could if we consolidated our purchasing clout to negotiate a price for the whole company rather than buy on a unit-by-unit basis. Sales representatives have limited authority on the prices they can quote, and we had to remove the autonomy of the unit manager in purchasing decisions. That responsibility was assumed by the corporate office, which could negotiate with the clout of five units instead of one.

By going directly to the purveyor's sales manager instead of to the sales representatives, we became what is called a "house account." As a result, sales reps no longer called upon individual locations. We were able to contact the sales manager of an "official supplier" whenever we had problems with deliveries or invoices; at the same time we were able to negotiate lower prices for all our units. That eliminated price and quality inconsistencies among units and lowered our overall food cost by 2 percent. And the approved suppliers benefited because our purchases from them increased.

For that system to work, however, you must establish product specifications for all items. A list of products should be sent to each supplier, who is then asked to indicate his best prices based on the premise that he will be given orders from all units within the system. In addition, price changes must be submitted to the corporate office at least one week before the increase takes effect; informing a unit manager of a price hike is not considered proper notice. That will give you time to check with other approved suppliers to determine if their prices are also lower. If so, unit managers should be notified weekly of the new low bid on specified items and allowed to switch suppliers for those items.

Under the system we had implemented in Kansas City, managers were no longer required to call around each week to get price quotations. They were responsible for "ordering" items from approved suppliers. They checked invoices for correct prices before forwarding them for payment. Couple those benefits with fewer deliveries and invoices to process and you see the benefits of consolidating your buying power.

1) Organizing your storage areas can increase the accuracy and speed up taking inventory.
   A. True
   B. False

(2) The more often you can get deliveries, the more inventory you need to keep on hand.
   A. True
   B. False

(3) Single par stock inventory levels are recommended in markets where you can get weekly deliveries.
   A. True
   B. False

(4) Multiple unit operations can consolidate their buying power by becoming a house account with their suppliers.
   A. True
   B. False

(5) When contact between the buyer and seller is made over the phone or face-to-face, it is referred to as open or informal buying.
   A. True
   B. False

ANSWERS: 1: A, 2: B, 3: B, 4: A, 5: A

Use the bid process to benefit your purchasing program

BUYING COMPETITIVELY requires knowing how prices for similar or identical products differ among purveyors. It is advantageous to obtain comparative price bids from a minimum of two purveyors to determine the range of prices and products available. Although you might think that price and quality are always directly related, that's not the case. High prices don't always equate to high quality, just as low prices don't necessarily mean low quality. That is especially true with fresh produce. When the price is the lowest — usually during peak growing season — the quality is the highest. When the price is high, the quality and consistency often are lacking.

The greater the probability of price or supply alterations, the greater the need to follow the market closely. Products previously considered stable in price, such as canned fruits and vegetables, are now subject to price changes, even after the season's crop has been processed, canned, and shipped to distributors. Fresh products of all types — such as fish, seafood, poultry, beef, pork, and produce — will fluctuate in price depending on weather events, shipping costs, product availability, and demand.

Obtaining bids from your suppliers is not a difficult undertaking. However, I must repeat that low price is not the only factor one should consider. If all things are equal between two suppliers — and they rarely are — the one with the lowest price gets the order. The truth is that suppliers are not equal in all areas of service, dependability, reliability, price, and product lines. Remember: Other considerations, such as credit terms, delivery frequency, minimum orders, and value-added services, also are critical to your purchasing decision and might be more important than just a low price.

A policy on substitutions must be included in your bids. Your specifications should state that prices be given only for specified brands or that only equivalent brands be substituted. If you have a preferred alternative to a specified brand, include that information. If you don't specify brands, you will need to describe quality characteristics or grades.

In addition, how you want the supplier to handle out-of-stock items must be stated. Some suppliers automatically substitute an item when it is out-of-stock and send the closest substitute. They do that primarily as a service to their customers, who can decide whether to accept or return the substituted brand or grade.

Develop a 'partnership' with each of your suppliers

12

CONSIDER RIGHT FROM THE BEGINNING that both parties in the buying transaction are dependent upon one another. In nature this type of relationship is referred to as *symbiosis*. It means "the consorting together of two dissimilar organisms in a mutually advantageous partnership."

Some manufacturers like General Mills and Pillsbury have integrated vertically into the foodservice business. And foodservice operators like Morrison's and McDonald's have integrated into the supplier side. But the majority of vendor-operator relationships can be described as symbiotic and one in which either side can end the relationship.

The relationship works best when both sides view the partnership in a mutually advantageous light. Sometimes one of the parties will approach the negotiating table and present unilateral demands and conditions to the other party. I'm not talking about product specifications here; I'm referring to such things as price guarantees and policies concerning credit, deliveries, and billing.

I'm not going to take sides. I've been involved in negotiations on both sides of the bargaining table. Obviously, in such negotiations both parties are attempting to get the most for their respective interests. But at times the attitude of the operators is heavily one-sided, based on the belief that unless they are tough, the purveyors will take advantage of them. And the attitude of some purveyors is that you cannot let operators get the upper hand for exactly the same reason.

Get to know your suppliers so that you're comfortable with them and trust what they tell you. However, as a check, periodically call around to other purveyors just to verify what you have been told. That isn't being sneaky or distrustful; it's just sound business sense. If a reliable source gave you a stock tip that sounded good, wouldn't you do some additional checking to verify the facts before you invested your money?

The foodservice operator who is inflexible regarding delivery times and days and wants to take his time paying off the account balance is just as unrealistic as the purveyor who sets the terms of ordering, delivery, returns, and credits without considering the needs of the client. The unreasonable operator seems to be saying, "If you want my business, this is what you must do for me, regardless of how it increases your distribution cost and disrupts your operating procedures." The other side of the coin is the autocratic vendor stating, "If you want us to service your account, this is what you have to do."

I assembled some suggestions that each operator might want to adopt to improve his relationship with the other. This is my advice. Don't be a fickle buyer who is penny-wise and dollar foolish. Look at your overall food bill, not just individual items. Value is determined by far more than price. Consider the extra services the purveyor provides, such as merchandising and marketing assistance, cooperative advertising, order summary reports, handling of credits and returns, special deliveries, and credit policy. The more business you do with a purveyor, the more important your account becomes, and the greater likelihood he will work with you to satisfy your special needs.

Pay your account on time to agreed-upon terms. The more frequently you pay, the lower you can negotiate the price. The longer you take to pay — or the longer the credit period — the higher the prices a supplier must charge. Think about it. Not too many businesses can get merchandise delivered to them to sell and not have to pay for it until a week later. Purveyors have the same demands on their cash flow as you.

Don't spread out your orders too thinly between suppliers of the same merchandise. Work to make your account an "A" or "B" rating. I know there are other factors, but it comes down to this: If a vendor meets your standards on a consistent basis and charges you a fair price, he deserves your business and your loyalty. You should not switch purveyors for a few cents per pound. Operators who have a history of dropping purveyors who don't have regard for their standards should also be loyal to vendors who serve them well. A good purveyor will treat the operator's interests like a true partner. For the truth is that it is in their best interest to do so. Support the vendors who work with you. Keep in mind that they're in business to make a profit, too, and when you require special considerations and services, that mutual loyalty will pay dividends.

What can purveyors do to improve their relationships with operators? First, they should be consistent with the ordering process, delivery schedules, product quality, and charge a fair price. They should look out for the operators' interests, not just their own. Purveyors should let operators know if items are in short supply, or that a price increase is imminent. Above all, they should protect their regular customers from shortages and allow them to benefit from special deals.

Maintain adequate stock levels of necessary products. When an item is in short supply, protect your clients' interests before selling to new accounts at higher profit levels. If prices are going to increase, give adequate notice. Be responsive to the particular needs of your clients and give them full benefit of your expertise in product knowledge, packaging, and distribution. When a restaurant operator entrusts you with his business, he should be treated with all due respect. The buyer and seller who are aware of each other's interests can work together for their mutual benefit.

13

What value-added services can you expect from your suppliers?

IF A GROUP OF RESTAURATEURS got together to discuss what they wanted from their suppliers, the following points very likely would be raised. Some operators would voice concerns about prices charged for specific items. Others would focus on the total cost of a purchasing program, not just individual products, contending that if they do more volume with a particular purveyor, they should receive better prices. With a streamlined purchasing program, cost efficiencies occur for both the operator and the supplier. In addition, less labor and less paperwork mean that more time can be devoted to customer-service issues.

Computerized controls and reports are part of the technological advances that make the ordering and billing process easier, more accurate, and more cost effective. Printouts of account activity and product usage can be obtained automatically. Such information is valuable to both the supplier and operator. If use levels are discovered to be substantial, additional price breaks may be negotiated.

A new process called Efficient Foodservice Response, or EFR, is being tested that supposedly will help operators work with their suppliers to eliminate inefficient practices and improve customer service. Various EFR studies estimate that at least 5 percent of all orders placed by operators with suppliers are erroneous. By placing orders electronically, order efficiency reportedly is improved, reducing the number of backorders and overstocking incidences. And while EFR is said to be at least three to four years away from being implemented nationwide, many suppliers already are taking orders via the Internet — a process that is expected to grow even more popular in the future.

Suppliers long have offered what has been referred to as "value-added services." They include new menu ideas, recipes, point-of-sales merchandising, staff training, and even product research and development. Some offer co-op advertising to defer costs of promotions and menu printing. Others can provide needed equipment if you purchase their products. Coffee suppliers are perhaps the most obvious example. Ice machines can be lent or leased at reasonable rates from your fountain syrup supplier. That can help you reduce the amount of your capital investment.

Some suppliers employ chefs and former managers who can help you and your staff develop new recipes or solve problems. Such services can be extremely valuable to independent operators.

Don't make overly restrictive demands on your purveyors

WHEN YOU SELECT A VENDOR to provide the products or services you need, don't make unilateral or unconditional demands in the negotiations. While you certainly should seek to optimize your restaurant's best interests, keep in mind that a more mutually beneficial solution will make both sides happy with the relationship.

We have all probably seen a sign on the delivery entrance stating, "No Deliveries Accepted Between 11:30 a.m. and 1:30 p.m." The rationale for the policy is evident: The busy lunch hour demands that all attention be focused on serving the customers. Nevertheless, we must look at policies like that from the purveyor's perspective, as well. Purveyors work to keep costs as low as possible so that their prices remain competitive and they earn additional profits. To help accomplish that, they route their delivery trucks in the most cost-efficient manner in an effort to minimize the mileage, increase the number of stops per route, and eliminate back-tracking.

Minimum-order quantities, billing procedures, and credit terms are also issues that must be negotiated. When it comes to payment terms, you must realize that the longer credit is extended to you, the higher the prices the purveyor must charge. If a purveyor is on COD or even prepayment terms with his suppliers, he cannot afford to give you 30 to 60 days to pay without charging more to compensate for the interest he incurs. Consequently, if you're paying COD or every seven days, you should be able to arrange better prices than someone else who has been extended credit for 30 days.

Remember: Purveyors are just as concerned with their cash flow as you are with yours. They have payrolls to meet, utilities, insurance premiums, and overhead, too. In other words, they have many of the same concerns about their business that you have for yours. That is especially true with the smaller independent specialty suppliers for meat, seafood, and produce. We have a tendency to think that the large full-line distributors like Rykoff-Sexton and Sysco are so big that they never have to be concerned with cash flow. The truth is that they have concerns when one or more of their largest accounts — usually regional or national chain accounts — hold back payments for even a few days.

So when it comes to an agreement that both parties are comfortable with, it makes for a more mutually beneficial relationship. You need to treat each other with respect and professionalism.

Why do suppliers impose minimum-order limits?

WHEN I WAS THE FOODSERVICE director for a small private college, I had a purveyor who would deliver six lemons if that was all I needed. I also have had suppliers who wouldn't deliver an order that was less than $250. That kind of disparity in delivery policies could be interpreted two ways. I can appreciate the gesture of the first supplier as an indication that he wanted our account. However, in the process of being competitive, a supplier still must contain delivery costs.

The wages of the delivery driver, the lease on the truck, maintenance, gas, and insurance are fixed costs that are pro-rated to every stop, no matter if it is for $4,000 or $4. A conservative, average cost per stop — based on the annual cost of putting a truck and driver on the road divided by the average number of deliver-

"The best way to predict the future is to invent it."

— ALAN KAY

---

ies made — is $50. Therefore, that cost must be allocated to the items being delivered. If a total of 10 cases of product are delivered, that adds $5 to the cost of each case or reduces the profit by $5 for each case. Contrast the delivery cost allocated over a 100-case order. That cost is now only 50 cents. It makes economic sense not to deliver where gross profit of the order doesn't cover the costs of the delivery.

With that in mind it should be clear that the more frequently deliveries are made to your establishment, the greater proportion of the fixed costs of delivery are being charged to you. That is why suppliers establish minimum-order quantities. Nevertheless, you always can find a supplier looking to gain a competitive advantage who will waive the minimum-order limit or simply not impose one.

Most of the time we make rules in our businesses for our benefit and to the detriment of customer service. Consider the coffee shop that serves three meals a day. Back when I was a general manager of a regional family restaurant chain, several of the line cooks complained that having to serve breakfast during the lunch and dinner hours was disruptive to getting the other orders out. We changed our menu and stopped serving breakfast at 11:00 a.m., much to the chagrin of some of our regular customers. Our rationalization was that it would make it easier on the cooks.

Limiting customer choices with no-substitution rules and other policies are often one-sided in favor of the restaurant and are usually imposed for the cause of cost and efficiency. However, operators often lose sight of how such changes will be viewed by the customers. Soon after we changed our breakfast policy, one of our competitors down the street noted that his business had begun to improve during the lunch hour. Several of our defecting customers told him that they were there because they still could order breakfast. So his new promotional slogan became, "Breakfast served anytime." It didn't matter that his cooks had to work a little harder; he welcomed the additional business. Eventually, we reversed our ill-advised decision.

That is the same kind of logic that sometimes drives rules and regulations imposed on operators by their suppliers. If purveyors place restrictions on ordering that require us to make major changes in the way we do things, we generally would just switch to another purveyor. As long as there are purveyors who are seeking to expand their business, overly restrictive delivery policies will not become standard industry practice unless tangible benefits can be shown to accrue to the buyer. Therefore, whenever restrictions are implemented, it behooves the supplier to demonstrate how the buyer will benefit by complying.

(1) The greater the probability of price or supply changes, the greater the need to follow the market closely.

   A. True
   B. False

(2) Low price is the determining factor one uses when selecting a purveyor.

   A. True
   B. False

(3) The purveyor-operator relationship works best when both sides view the arrangement as a mutually advantageous partnership.

   A. True
   B. False

(4) Which of the following are "value-added services?"

   A. Computerized ordering and billing
   B. New menu ideas
   C. Point-of-sale merchandise
   D. Co-op advertising
   E. All of the above

(5) Mutual respect and understanding of each others' needs and concerns must be present for the purveyor-operator relationship to work effectively.

   A. True
   B. False

ANSWERS: 1: A, 2: B, 3: A, 4: E, 5: A

Develop a routine and system for your accounts payable

16

WHEN IT COMES TIME TO PAY the bills at the end of the month, the invoice is your most important piece of paper. One rule you should follow strictly is: "Pay from invoices, not statements." Statements are mailed out at the end of the supplier's accounting cycle, which may not always be compatible with yours. Typically, most of us keep our books on a monthly accounting period, while suppliers close their books before the last day of the month. As a result, you might have a delivery come in after the statement date. While that technically gives you more time to pay that last invoice, it is part of your closing month's expenses and must be recorded. There are also times when your accounting period ends and the supplier sends a statement that includes an invoice that should be charged to the following month. Given that

> **"Destiny is not a matter of chance, it is a matter of choice; it is not a thing to be waited for, it is a thing to be achieved."**
>
> — WILLIAM JENNINGS BRYAN

---

you are likely dealing with around 20 different suppliers with different billing procedures, you must organize your accounts payable procedures.

The only way to keep all of that straight is to pay from invoices, not from monthly statements. In addition, given the credits and returns that usually occur, statements might not reflect all of the credits you are due. However, if the invoices have been checked and credit memorandums attached, proper account balances can be determined. Many times credit memos issued by your sales representative have not been entered into your account. When I opened my first restaurant, a sales representative instructed me to pay the full invoice amount, and he would issue a credit that would be reflected on my next statement. I remember how I worried that I would forget about the credit. From that point on I always took any credit when I paid my invoices and let the supplier's accounting procedures catch up to my adjusted balance.

All of your bills should be paid by check. Journal and ledger entries can be made from the transactions indicated in your check register. Cash payouts are recorded on a separate form so they can be entered. With your inventory and purchase amounts, your accountant can prepare your monthly income statements with any basic accounting software.

The checks used in your general account where you deposit your daily sales revenues should have a section in which to indicate the invoice numbers you're paying. It is extremely important to have that information on your check because it will allow you to prove that you have paid a particular invoice if your account balance ever is disputed. You should also indicate the number of the check on each invoice. That simply entails writing "Paid Check No. 123" on the top invoice of a group you have stapled together. With those two steps you can now trace a check to an invoice and an invoice to a check.

If you cannot produce an invoice, it probably means you haven't paid it. Ask for a copy of the unpaid invoice from your supplier to see if it contains the necessary authorization. Once our produce supplier called to tell me that we had one invoice outstanding for about four months. I couldn't find the invoice in my "paid" invoices, so I asked for a copy. The copy contained the name of our restaurant, but it hadn't been signed by any of our employees. We also learned that it was a "dock-pick up," not a restaurant delivery. We successfully proved that the mistake was theirs, not ours. The fact that we had an excellent payment history certainly had a lot to do with the purveyor's resolving it in our favor by issuing a credit.

What about discovering errors after the goods have been received and even used? That often happens when you're extending invoices and discover a pricing discrepancy. You can still deduct for the credit and simply attach a credit memorandum to your check. Believe me, your purveyor's accounts-receivable clerk appreciates the little note that explains why you took a credit. Without that, you will receive a call asking why you paid less than the amount shown on the invoice or statement.

Evaluating potential suppliers

THERE PROBABLY ARE many food, beverage, supply, and equipment dealers serving your city. And because you can't deal with every one of them, the ones who want your business will call upon you. That is an advantageous position to be in because it improves your bargaining position. You can negotiate for better prices and services when there are two or more suppliers seeking your account. Even after you've made your choices, suppliers will work to gain an increasing proportion of your order so that their competitors will get less.

Consequently, you should expect supplier representatives to make "cold calls" to your place of business — that is, just stopping in early in the week when they know most operators are preparing their weekly orders. Initially, they will just stop by to introduce themselves

> **"Genius is perseverance in disguise."**
>
> — MIKE NEWLINE

and their company, give you a product list, and ask some questions about the products you buy. The next week they might stop in, quote you prices on some items, and ask if you would like to give them a trial order. Many times they will quote you a "low-ball price" just to get you to order.

A good supplier representative will conduct some research on your restaurant before he or she calls upon you. The rep should have a clear understanding of your restaurant's identity, your menu, and what you are noted for. To gather that information, the rep can question colleagues, get a copy of your menu, or simply eat in your restaurant. Once he's in the restaurant, additional information can be gathered from your employees. The more information sales reps have, the more directly they can discuss your needs.

Avoid dealing with uninformed sales representatives. If they don't have specific product knowledge and an understanding of your business, they will use only the low-price sales pitch to win your business. That rep loses credibility with me as well as the possibility of any future transactions.

In most cases the sales representative knows his business better than you know yours. He knows the market for his product lines, the forecasted supply, and the current demand. He knows who his competition is for your business, what they charge, and what the market will support. After all, they likely are obtaining their inventory from many of the same canners, packers, and brokers.

If you're loyal to your regular suppliers, you won't be switching your orders to another supplier for just a lower price. You should request information about the supplier, such as whether is he financially sound and dependable. You can even request references. Ask him to provide names of restaurants and institutions he has been selling to for more than six months.

If you're really interested in changing suppliers, arrange a tour of the warehouse or processing plant. You can tell a lot when you see how organized, clean, and efficient the supplier's operations are. You must discuss delivery schedules and payment policy. The professionalism and personality of the sales representative also will play a large part in giving the "new" supplier a trial order. I believe suppliers respect owners and managers who deal with them this way because they realize that if they earn your loyalty, you will not capriciously switch to the next supplier who calls with a better price. Your assessment of a supplier takes more into account that just the prices they charge.

(1) To keep your billing to suppliers manageable and organized, you should pay from invoices, not statements.

    A. True
    B. False

(2) By noting the invoice numbers on your checks and the check numbers on paid invoices, you can cross-reference payments and invoices whenever account balances are in dispute.

    A. True
    B. False

(3) You can usually negotiate a more competitive price and get better service when more than one supplier is bidding for your account.

    A. True
    B. False

(4) It is not necessary for a restaurant operator to ask for references when a new supplier representative makes a cold call.

    A. True
    B. False

(5) A good sales representative will do some research about your restaurant before he or she calls upon you.

    A. True
    B. False

ANSWERS: 1: A, 2: A, 3: A, 4: B, 5: A

18

Know the role of the sales representative in the business relationship

WHILE MOST FRANCHISES and chains have national-account status with major suppliers, unit managers still must have face-to-face — or ear-to-ear — contact with the person who services their account. There needs to be someone who can be contacted in the event of a problem. Independent restaurant operators deal primarily with and through the supplier representative. Approximately 45 percent of the 608,000 commercial restaurants in the United States are sole proprietorships or partnerships, while another 25 percent are independently operated corporations. That means that about 425,000 locations are being called upon by supplier sales representatives who establish close working relationships with many of the owners and managers. They not only take their weekly order; they also may receive payment of past invoices,

> **"If the highest aim of a captain were to preserve his ship, he would keep it in port forever."**
>
> — THOMAS AQUINAS

provide the operator with specific product knowledge, market information about future supply and price, introduce the operator to new products and brands, and even make emergency deliveries.

I recall one sales representative for a dish detergent company who would come out on a Friday night to fix my dishwasher in the middle of the dinner period. On another occasion we ran out of dish detergent before our replacement order arrived, and he brought us a case of detergent to get us through until our shipment arrived. I asked him where he got it because I know he didn't keep stock at his office, and he said he borrowed a case from another one of his clients. When our order arrived, he picked up a case and returned it to the restaurant he had borrowed it from.

Sales representatives must be more than mere order-takers. He has to know your business and keep your best interests in mind at all times. You want a sales representative who is honest and open with you about price and supply. He should never promise anything that he cannot deliver. Before taking your order, he should be knowledgeable of any stock-outs and pending price increases. He should inform you whenever certain conditions or changes will affect items you purchase. When a product is in short supply, he should make certain his regular customers receive his orders before those items are offered to new customers.

Your sales rep takes your concerns, complaints, and requests to the company. He can help you extend your payment of invoices when you have a major insurance or tax obligation to meet. He can write the credit memorandums when you return merchandise or when there is a price extension dispute. It makes a difference when you have a problem that requires an adjustment to your account, and it is handled quickly and without a series of questions that imply that you are trying to put one over on him.

The supplier filling the order is not always the one with the lowest price. If the price advantage is neutralized, the decision on whom to order from will be based on such factors as service and value-added benefits. For that reason the sales representative must be much more than just an order-taker.

(1) The majority of restaurants in the U.S. have sales representatives call upon the owner or manager to obtain their weekly orders.

A. True
B. False

(2) Chains and franchise operations that establish national accounts with certain suppliers don't need to have personal contact with a supplier representative to service their accounts.

A. True
B. False

(3) A good sales representative takes your concerns, complaints, and requests to the company and argues on your behalf.

A. True
B. False

(4) Which of the following is the least important function of the sales representative to the restaurant owner or manager?

A. Takes the weekly order
B. Collects payment of past invoices
C. Provides the operator with specific product knowledge
D. Provides market information about future supply and price
E. Makes emergency deliveries when needed

(5) Storage space is the major consideration in determining the amount of inventory kept on hand.

A. True
B. False

ANSWERS: 1: A, 2: B, 3: A, 4: B, 5: B

How many suppliers should you use?

THIS DECISION SHOULD BE based largely on how many potential suppliers it takes to fill your purchase specifications and the amount of weekly or monthly purchases you make on a regular basis. Over the past 15 years, the large national chain operators have been working to reduce the number of suppliers they deal with regularly. As suppliers and distributors merge with other regional and local distributors, the delivery area they service has grown considerably. That has allowed chains to consolidate their purchasing power by establishing national accounts with distributors who can service all of their stores. As a direct result, both product costs for the restaurant operators and distribution costs for the suppliers have decreased.

Having fewer suppliers makes sense because it helps chains gain cost and quality

"One hundred percent of the shots you don't take don't go in."

— WAYNE GRETZKY

---

consistency and reduces the processing costs of accounts payable. One national foodservice operator discovered that it was writing checks each month to more than 635 different suppliers. Since then the company has consolidated its buying and reduced that number to less than 150. Consider the savings alone on processing invoices and writing checks that resulted from that single decision.

Another consideration in your decision on how many suppliers to use is the total dollar amount of purchases you regularly make in a given food category, such as dairy, meat, or produce. Typically, one doesn't require more than one dairy supplier because the amount ordered is limited, and if that were split between two or more suppliers, it would not be a profitable stop for the supplier. Suppliers will "grade" their accounts based on purchase amounts, payment history, returns, and delivery issues. They seek to have all "A" accounts — that is, those that purchase well above minimum-order quantities on a regular basis, pay their invoices on time, and don't have an excessive number of returns or restrictive delivery policies.

Consequently, as an operator, you get the best service and prices when your accounts grade out as an "A" or "B." If you split your orders too thinly, you become a marginal "B" or even a "C" grade account and eventually you will find that the supplier will begin to view you as a marginal account.

I would recommend that you always have a "back-up" supplier for items that are extremely important to your business. In those cases it is recommended that you have a secondary supplier that you deal with every week in addition to your primary supplier. If a critical product is available from only one supplier, and you purchase large quantities, you might want to convince a second supplier to carry it as well. That provides you with a backup so that you will have an alternative source. That practice also keeps suppliers on their toes with prices and service, since they see the potential to increase their share of your order each week.

(1) A multi-unit chain would more likely use multiple specialty purveyors to service its locations rather than a "total supplier."

    A. True

    B. False

(2) When calculating the amount of each item to order, you need to consider:

    A. The use levels between deliveries

    B. The amount presently on hand

    C. The minimum inventory needed as a safety factor

    D. The frequency of deliveries

    E. All of the above

(3) There has been a movement over the past several years to increase the number of suppliers rather than reduce them.

    A. True

    B. False

(4) Having fewer suppliers assists chains in obtaining cost and quality consistency and reduce their accounts payable costs as well.

    A. True

    B. False

(5) You get the best prices and services when your account is graded as an "A" or "B" by your supplier.

    A. True

    B. False

ANSWERS: 1: B, 2: E, 3: B, 4: A, 5: A

20

Develop your own purchase specifications

YOU MUST HAVE SPECIFICATIONS for every product you purchase. Developing purchasing specs is like developing operating and personnel policy: They're best when based on recurring situations and decisions made in the course of the daily business activity. It is not surprising that operators have a tendency to purchase brands and products they know and like. Similarly, products that did not work out are avoided, regardless of price breaks. Over time a particular grade, size, brand, or variety of meat, produce, fresh, canned or frozen product becomes the preferred one, sometimes by default. I use that term in the way it is used for computer software — unless you configure your software differently, it will always default to the programmed setting.

Specifications set by default aren't necessarily written down; nevertheless, they are just as formal as a written specification in a franchise chain operator's manual. In fact, the presence of a written specification is not the element that makes it a formal spec, but rather what is regularly ordered from a supplier. For example, an independent restaurant operator who insists on using only a certain brand of mayonnaise for her homemade tartar sauce and blue cheese dressing has established a purchase specification for mayonnaise by default. A franchise chain will specify the particular brand of mayonnaise that suppliers cannot substitute, but the default specification of the independent operator is no less formal than that of the franchise operation.

It's just as important to have specifications when you're a single-unit independent operation. In order to establish some competitive distinctiveness in the marketplace, every restaurant must have several house specialties or signature items. Those items are prepared following standardized recipes the owner or chef would never consider changing. If a barbecue sauce recipe starts with Cattleman's barbecue sauce as the base, to which is added Lea & Perrins Worcestershire sauce, French's Dijon mustard, Wishbone Italian salad dressing, and Tony Chachere's Creole Seasoning, substitute brands of those ingredients won't be used, regardless of the price.

A restaurant that specializes in Prime rib will discover over time the best-quality grade, yield grade, and weight of the rib that results in the greatest yield. After hundreds of ribs have been roasted, a specification will become evident. In addition, one may specify that the rib come from Iowa Beef Packers and even specify Certified Black Angus breed.

Typically, a purchase specification will include the following: (1) trade name or common name of the product; (2) quantity in a case, pound, or carton, and unit size on which the price is quoted; (3) trade or federal grade; (4) size of the container/packaging; (5) other descriptors, such as geographic origin (Florida grapefruit), variety (Idaho russet potato), style (solid-pack pie apples), count or size (5x6 tomatoes), condition upon receipt (fresh, frozen), and any other descriptive terms that define possible choices.

Specifications are required because considerable differences exist between brands of products like mayonnaise, barbecue sauces, and salad dressings. You cannot just ask for "canned green beans in No. 10 cans." You must include the USDA grade, such as Fancy, Extra Standard, or Standard. You also must state the variety of bean — Blue Lake, Kentucky, Wonder, Tendergreen — and the types — round, flat, pole, or bush. In addition, you can specify the growing area — Northwest, Midwest, Mid-Atlantic — as well as the pack — whole, vertical pack, French cut, cut, and short cut.

Obviously, there are numerous choices of brands and grades for all food products purchased by a commercial and institutional foodservice operation. While there are standards of identity for products like peanut butter, fruit cocktail, catsup, pancake syrup, different brands of the same product will not perform or taste the same when incorporated into your recipes.

Finally, product specifications serve another purpose than taste and quality consistency in standardized recipes. They also help establish cost consistency in our menu items. When prices are quoted by your suppliers, they will be quoting on identical products. When you make the purchasing decision as to who will be your approved supplier, both price and quality will be consistent.

What is the 'best' price?

THE "BEST" PRICE is not necessarily the "lowest" price. With most products we buy, a direct correlation exists between price and quality. Low prices on some items are associated with lower quality, such as meat and seafood. However, in other situations, it can be just the opposite — for example, produce during peak growing season. The more one pays for any product or service, the greater the buyer's expectations will be for quality and service after the sale.

A restaurant operator must purchase raw materials and process them for sale to the public. Direct costs are incurred, and a sizable investment in a physical plant and equipment is made. Given the time, effort, expertise, investment, and risk operators take, they are entitled to a profit for their effort. That justifies the markup over cost for their products and ser-

> **"Any business arrangement that is not profitable to the other person will in the end prove unprofitable for you. The bargain that yields mutual satisfaction is the only one that is apt to be repeated."**
>
> — B.C. FORBES

vices. Suppliers have the same financial goals and a right to make a profit for all of their effort and risk.

Prices charged cannot be determined exclusively by a simple markup over cost. Competitive forces in the marketplace limit what can be charged for any given product or service. It is said that the buyer, not the seller, has the final say in what price to charge. Nothing is worth more than the price someone is willing to pay. So, basically, cost plays an important but limited role in the pricing decision. It comes down to whether the supplier can sell the product or service at a price acceptable to the buyer and still make a reasonable profit.

The "best" price is therefore not necessarily the "lowest" price, but rather the price that provides the best overall value. Value is a feeling that one has received his or her money's worth in terms of quality, quantity, and service.

Remember: We usually get what we pay for. The disappointment and dissatisfaction of realizing that you have purchased an inferior product or service remains long after the brief exhilaration from having paid a cheap price is gone. And in the case of a restaurant customer, the taste of a bad meal lingers long after the initial satisfaction of redeeming a two-for-one coupon.

Many state and national governmental agencies still are required by statute to purchase based on the lowest bid. While that process works well with computers and office copiers, it is problematic when it comes to food products and food distributors and often causes problems with the quality of the goods and services those operators ultimately receive. On the other hand, it can be effective in situations where branded products are specified and service after the delivery is not a factor.

If you specify high quality, you can expect to pay higher prices. However, paying low prices does not always translate into savings. When excessive trim loss results from preparing produce, beef, or seafood, the actual cost-per-servable pound can be double the as-purchased price. For example, a restaurant owner who refused to purchase from the local seafood distributor and instead contracted with a commercial fisherman, was paying $6 per pound for whole, dressed grouper. He had the fish filleted and delivered to the restaurant, less the head and bones. The yield was 50 percent of the weight of the whole, dressed fish. Consequently, the "real" cost per servable pound was not $6, but $12. In addition, he had to take the entire catch — regardless of whether the quantity was greater than what the restaurant could expect to sell before it turned bad. The price of grouper fillets from the local seafood supplier was considerably less than $8 per pound, and the restaurateur could order only what was required. Therefore, true value encompasses far more than paying a low price.

How much should you keep in inventory?

I WAS ASKED THIS QUESTION during an interview for my first teaching job. I was interviewing before graduation from the MBA program at Michigan State University, where I majored in hotel, restaurant, and institutional management. I was a 23-year-old candidate for the chairman of the restaurant management program at a junior college in Kansas City, Mo., and I was being interviewed by the dean of the vocational-technical division and the president of the college.

The president explained that he came from a private women's college in downstate Missouri. The school fed 500 students three meals a day, seven days a week, and it budgeted $5 per student per day for meals. He asked me, "How much inventory would you keep on hand?" I vividly recall that I started to do some

> **"If you don't know where you are going, you will probably end up somewhere else."**
>
> — LAWRENCE J. PETER

quick math in my head. Five hundred times $5 times seven days, add at least four days as a safety factor, 40 percent food cost — and then it came to me. He wasn't expecting me to give him a dollar figure; he wanted a general response. So I answered, "As little as possible."

I explained that the dollar amount and quantities would depend on such things as the frequency of deliveries, storage space, product perishability, minimum-order requirements, market dynamics, quantity discounts, and payment terms. The president went on to say that his former college incurred a rather serious short-term cash-flow deficit when the director of foodservice presented the treasurer with an invoice for $12,000 worth of food inventory that had been delivered.

The point of the story is that you don't want to convert your liquid cash into perishable food inventory if you can help it. The more frequently you can get deliveries from your suppliers, the less inventory you must keep on hand. In fact, Houston's Restaurants is testing a "no-inventory" system in several of its restaurants. The units have reduced the amount of inventory and are receiving daily deliveries from purveyors. Basically, it is a cash-management strategy that results in increased liquidity for the company. Preliminary results suggest that food costs are more easily controlled because units are given an allowance on how much they purchase from each food group based on a percentage of food sales. For example, each unit can spend 20 percent on produce, 25 percent on red meats, and 12 percent on dry and canned goods.

Purchases should be tied directly to sales and not storage capacity or some par-stock level based on the maximum usage plus a safety factor. The use level between deliveries is the factor that determines the amount you must keep on hand. If you get only one delivery each week, your average inventory should never be more than a 10-day supply. If you receive deliveries twice a week, the inventory can be reduced to a five-day supply. Exceptions can occur when special purchases are made to take advantage of a great price. You also might increase inventory if a product is in short supply, and you wanted to ensure that you had enough to meet your needs.

You want to have a high inventory turnover, and a rule of thumb is three times per month. The figure is calculated by dividing your cost of food consumed by your average inventory. Cost of food consumed is found by adding beginning inventory and purchases and then subtracting your ending inventory. Average inventory is simply the average of your opening and ending inventory. If you divide the turnover rate into 30 days, it will give you the number of days' supply you're averaging in your inventory at any given time during the month.

23

What do you do if an indispensable product is going to be in short supply and likely to increase in price?

DO YOU RECALL the tomato-product shortage that occurred in the mid-1970s? If you were in business then, you probably remember that all tomato products, from catsup to barbecue sauce, not only increased significantly in price but also became harder to find as the months went on. I had just opened my first operation, an Italian restaurant that used considerable quantities of canned whole tomatoes, tomato sauce, and tomato paste. I recall that the cost of tomato paste went from around $12 for a case of No. 10 cans to more than $24. The change was so extreme that we altered our standardized recipe and replaced one can of paste with one can of extraheavy tomato puree.

When my Italian import specialty supplier informed me that he could get 400 cases of tomato products for me at close to what the

> **"Even if you're on the right track, you'll get run over if you just sit there."**
>
> — WILL ROGERS

restaurant originally was paying, I obviously was interested. He told me that I would have to take delivery and pay for them within 30 days. Fortunately, we were in a financial position to take advantage of the offer. But because we didn't have space in our restaurant, I had them delivered to my home and stored in my garage.

The reason I decided to make the purchase was twofold. First, the price was exceptional compared with what we would pay on the spot market. And second, there was no guarantee that we could get an adequate supply on the open market. I guessed right that year — tomato product prices continued to rise. Domestic packs were entirely consumed, and distributors were forced to resort to imported tomato products from Israel, Spain, and Italy, all of which sold for considerably higher prices than domestic brands.

The next year my supplier came to me and asked if I wanted to purchase another 400 cases. I asked him about the supply and price forecast for the next year. He replied that supply was steady, and price might increase by only 50 cents per case at the most. With supply assured and a minimal price increase expected, I opted to take my chances with open-market buying.

I finally negotiated a consignment inventory deal. The same supplier offered to purchase 400 cases at a set price and store them for me in his warehouse. I would be billed for what was shipped each week with our regular order. I always wondered why the supplier didn't offer me the same deal the year before. We did, however, switch to the supplier's label on the tomato products. Since the price the supplier paid was based on how many cases it ordered of its private label, it was able to increase its order (and get a better price). Our agreement to purchase 400 cases guaranteed that it would sell a significant portion of its inventory.

Consignment is much preferred to having to make payment in advance. The first time we basically converted our liquid cash into perishable food inventory. It is much easier to control your cash in a savings or checking account than inventory in your storerooms and walk-ins. The moral of this story is to avoid tying up your cash in food inventory unless product availability is extremely uncertain and the products are critical to your operation. If supply is stable, take your chances on the open market. You can still stock up on exceptionally good buys or look for a consignment deal.

(1) Product specifications are an important element of your food cost and quality-control standards.

A. True
B. False

(2) You cannot have effective purchase specifications if they are not put in writing.

A. True
B. False

(3) Which of the following is not part of a product specification?

A. Trade name of the product
B. Trade or federal grade
C. Condition upon receipt
D. The standardized recipe
E. Quantity in a case, pound, or carton

(4) The lowest price is always the best price.

A. True
B. False

(5) Paying low prices does not always translate into savings and value.

A. True
B. False

ANSWERS: 1: A, 2: B, 3: D, 4: B, 5: A

24

Electronic inventory and order systems: Yours or theirs?

THE PERSONAL COMPUTER has become an essential tool for cost-control and inventory management. Despite the technological advances only a relatively small number of restaurants have implemented software programs. The use of computer software to manage inventories and sales analysis is required more for competitive survival than for its labor-savings benefits. This is the "age of information," and those with the most information have a distinct advantage.

Suppliers have embraced electronic technology in the management of their business and accounts. Many have gone online so that their sales representatives now carry laptop computers that allow them to transmit orders, check account balances, obtain purchase history, inventory quantities, and monitor prices and deliveries through a modem. Buyers can con-

> **"Getting results through people is a skill that cannot be learned in the classroom."**
>
> — J. Paul Getty

---

nect to a supplier Web page and download product information and even place orders electronically. In some cases invoices and payments are made electronically, resulting in cost savings in the processing of accounts receivable and accounts payable.

Progressive restaurateurs are investing in point-of-sale computers that not only track their sales by menu item but also are tied to inventory usage. Each time a menu item is sold, the ingredients used are subtracted from inventory in quantities stated on a standardized recipe. The use levels are compared with the actual number sold. At the end of the month, the program can print out a variance report flagging inventory items that indicate where actual use levels exceed the standard. That alerts management to potential portioning, theft, and waste problems.

Several benefits accrue from electronic automation. In addition to the information that such systems provide, they decrease the time spent by management in the ordering and inventory functions. Keep in mind that those systems are only as good as the information they contain. You must understand that someone on your staff has to enter the information from delivery invoices on a daily basis. Eventually, that will be accomplished via the Internet or with the scanning of Universal Product Codes.

Operators seeking to move forward with the latest software technology have two choices. They can use the software provided by their food distributor, or they can purchase software from an independent provider. When you're dealing with multiple suppliers, having to work with more than one software program can be problematic. Therefore, it would be better for your suppliers to adapt to your in-house system. Just be certain that your software has the capability of interfacing with their software.

If you're an "A" account, your supplier even might offer to give you a personal computer to run the program as part of the deal. Such "connections" can cement the partnership, although it is really a "marriage" of sorts in which separation can be disruptive to both parties. If you enter into that kind of relationship, you will be limiting your purchasing authority. The automation is a cost and time-saving tool, not just a functional transfer of data. If you are apprehensive about computers but feel the need to use them, move gradually. Start with just one of your suppliers and see how it works.

(1) The personal computer has become an essential tool for cost control and inventory management.

   A. True
   B. False

(2) Computerized inventory records are replacing the manually prepared inventory book.

   A. True
   B. False

(3) Automation of inventory is diminishing the need for any "personal relationship" with your supplier.

   A. True
   B. False

(4) Quantity discounts and early payment of invoices should always be taken when offered.

   A. True
   B. False

(5) Many restaurant operators use their suppliers to budget their monthly expenses by simply delaying payment of invoices for a few weeks.

   A. True
   B. False

ANSWERS: 1: A, 2: A, 3: B, 4: B, 5: A

Are quantity discounts worth the savings?

SHOULD YOU TAKE ADVANTAGE of quantity discounts? Should you pay your bill early to obtain the prepayment discount if offered? There are two schools of thought on that one. You can certainly calculate the amount of overpayment you are making when you fail to pay your bills in time to earn a discount or the savings you've lost by purchasing in small lots that don't qualify you for a discount. But many times our cash position, use levels, and storage space do not permit early payment or quantity purchases.

Keep repeating to yourself that it's much easier to maintain control of your cash when it's in the bank than if it's tied up in food or beverage inventory. Moreover, small savings are not always worth the loss of a liquid cash position, especially when you have more pressing needs for that cash. Many restaurant operators use suppliers to budget their monthly expenses. Instead of borrowing money from the bank, they simply hold off paying a supplier for a few weeks.

If the cost of borrowing $1,000 is 12-percent simple interest, and a late payment to a supplier doesn't impose any interest penalty, why not take advantage of that interest-free loan? Ask yourself, "What is the incentive to a supplier who offers you a deal that if you buy 10 cases, you get one free?" If you normally purchase only four cases a month and then suddenly are required to purchase 10, your supplier has converted his inventory into cash, and you now have tied up more than twice as much of your cash in inventory. It will take you two months to recover the money, and you won't see any gross profit until the last few cases are sold. That is referred to in accounting as the cash-to-cash cycle. You went from a 30-day cycle to a 60-day cycle.

I recall running into my accountant at the airport one month after I opened my first restaurant. I told him proudly that we had paid all of our bills for the previous month before the 15th of the month. I thought he would congratulate me, but instead he replied, "Why did you do that?" He asked if we had earned any discounts for early payment, and if the prices would be increased if we paid them off within 30 days instead of 14. I answered "no" to both questions.

He then explained that it might be better to hold on to our cash a little longer and utilize the "float" that we had between depositing sales and paying our bills. That strategy was demonstrated to me several months later in a conversation with our meat supplier sales representative. He was excited about landing a new fast-food hamburger chain account for all of its ground beef. However, his attitude changed dramatically when, 90 days later, the chain had not paid any of its account, which at that point totaled more than $45,000. The chain was using that supplier's money to improve its cash position and for financing additional locations. The meat supplier eventually got his money but declined to supply the chain in the future because of the strain its slow payment placed on cash flow.

Discounts for full-case lots also are offered by liquor distributors as an incentive to not break cases or purchase single bottles. When it comes to certain premium brands of single-malt scotches or liquors, a single bottle can run more than $40 or $50, and it could take months before a case would be sold. Consequently, that could mean tying up more than $600 of your cash for just a single case of liquor. As an incentive, distributors offer a 10-percent discount if you purchase a case so you only tie up $540 for 12 bottles. If you do that with a dozen brands, you will be tying up several thousand dollars in inventory. If you're like me, I would rather pay a little more to keep my liquidity position strong. So consider those things when you're being offered a quantity discount.

DAVE PAVESIC is a former restaurateur who now teaches hospitality administration at the university level. He previously owned and operated two casual-theme Italian restaurants in Orlando, Fla.; served as general manager of operations of a six-unit regional chain in the Midwest, operating four coffee shops, a fine-dining seafood restaurant and one drive-in; and was a college foodservice director. He currently teaches courses on restaurant cost control, financial management, and food production in the Cecil B. Day School of Hospitality Administration at Georgia State University in Atlanta, Ga. He has written numerous articles on menu-sales analysis, labor cost, menu pricing and equipment layout. His two other books are *The Fundamental Principles of Restaurant Cost Control*, Prentice Hall Publishers, 1998, ISBN 0-13-747999-9 and *Menu Pricing and Strategy*, fourth edition, Van Nostrand Reinhold Publishers, 1996, ISBN 0-471-28747-4.